A Few Masonic Sermons

By

A. C. Ward and Bascom B. Clarke

Copyright © 2020 Lamp of Trismegistus. All rights reserved. No part of this publication may be reproduced or transmitted in any form or by any means, electronic or mechanical, including photocopying, recording, or by any information storage and retrieval system, without permission in writing from Lamp of Trismegistus. Reviewers may quote brief passages.

ISBN: 978-1-63118-435-2

*Foundations of Freemasonry
Series*

Other Books in this Series and Related Titles

A Few More Masonic Sermons
by T. E. Poole & Bascom B. Clarke (978-1-63118-436-9)

Royal Arch, Capitular and Cryptic Masonry
by various authors (978-1-63118-425-3)

Masonic Symbolism of Easter and the Christ in Masonry
by various authors (978-1-63118-434-5)

Masonic Symbolism of King Solomon's Temple
by Albert G. Mackey, David Harlow & Robert Smailes
(978-1-63118-442-0)

Psalms of Solomon by King Solomon (978-1-63118-439-0)

The Two Great Pillars of Boaz and Jachin
by Albert G. Mackey, H. L. Haywood, William Harvey & others
(978-1-63118-433-8)

Masonic Symbolism of the Apron & the Altar
by various authors (978-1-63118-428-4)

Lost Chapters of the Book of Daniel and Related Writings
by Daniel (978-1-63118-417-8)

Cloud Upon the Sanctuary by K. Eckartshausen (978-1-63118-438-3)

Symbolism and Discourses on the Entered Apprentice, Fellowcraft and Master Mason Blue Lodge Degrees by various (978-1-63118-413-0)

The Lost Keys of Freemasonry or The Secret of Hiram Abiff
by Manly P. Hall (978-1-63118-427-7)

The Story and Legend of Hiram Abiff by William Harvey, Manly P. Hall & Albert G. Mackey (978-1-63118-411-6)

Audio Versions are also Available on Audible and iTunes

Table of Contents

Introduction...7

A Masonic Sermon
by A. C. Ward...9

Note...17

A Sermon About the Perception of Truth
by Bascom B. Clarke...19

A Sermon on Humility
by Bascom B. Clarke...23

A Sermon on Obligations
by Bascom B. Clarke ...27

A Sermon on Building Character
by Bascom B. Clarke...31

A Sermon on Honor
by Bascom B. Clarke...35

A Sermon on Acting Squarely
by Bascom B. Clarke...39

A Sermon on Forgiveness
by Bascom B. Clarke...43

True Spirit of the Craft
by Bascom B. Clarke...47

A Sermon on Tolerance
by Bascom B. Clarke...49

Introduction

From the beginning of Modern Freemasonry's birthdate of 1717, the intelligentsia of humanity have found refuge for safe reflection within the walls of the fraternity. Masonic writers have produced a nearly incalculable amount of written musings on a multitude of esoteric and philosophical subjects, as they relate to the ancient mysteries that Freemasonry currently storehouses. Sadly, most of it appears to have sat largely unread, as American Freemasonry in particular, continues to transform itself into something that bears little resemblance to what it was originally designed to be. The true essence of Freemasonry is not that of blind patriotism or a single-minded national religion but one of Universal Brotherhood and altruism, designed for the betterment not just of its members but of society as a whole. In particular, for those who are not members of the fraternity, as Freemasonry has always acted as a beacon, to help guide humanity through darker times, with the hopes that one day we will collectively reach a truly enlightened age.

It's not uncommon for new members joining the fraternity to find little education within the walls of many modern lodges, in spite of so much written material available to the membership. Many older members are not simply uneducated with regards to real Masonic history and symbology, not to mention the vast arena of related subjects, but they are disinterested in all of it, as well.

Lamp of Trismegistus is doing its part to help preserve humanity's Masonic history by making some of these classics available to those students who are seeking to unearth the knowledge of these ancient colossi. As such, Lamp of Trismegistus offers its readers highlights of Masonic study, culled from a variety of authors and viewpoints, with the hope bringing education back into the fraternity. So, be sure to check out other titles in our *Foundations of Freemasonry Series* as well as our *Esoteric Classics*, *Theosophical Classics*, *Occult Fiction* and our *Christian Apocrypha Series*, and don't be afraid to let a little altruism into your own heart or even into your Lodge. You can also download the audio versions of most of these titles from iTunes or Audible, for learning on the go.

A Masonic Sermon

By A. C. Ward

"God said let there be light and there was light."

Our text is the beginning of time on earth. As to how long this earth and all created things about us lay sleeping in the shroud of darkness and inactivity it is necessary for us to conjecture. Suffice for us to know that in the fullness of time while darkness was upon the face of the deep God said light be and light was. From that day to the present man has ever been in search of *more light*. Born into an existence, which is surrounded by mystery, we are constantly being overtaken and made to stumble in our blundering and mistakes. Like a blind man we know not how near we may be to the edge of a fearful pitfall. We only know that for the present moment our feet seem to rest on solid ground. We can only blindly feel our way, never knowing what a day or an hour may bring forth. Life is a game. An ill move may bring defeat while the slightest gain, a single word or act, may ensure a victory. Our knowledge of today may become the ignorance of tomorrow. The very things which we pass judgment upon today may be the acts which we ourselves may be guilty of the next day.

We can never grasp a certain point in human knowledge and say, "this I know!" We know absolutely nothing as to our origin, our destiny. In the providence of God our lives are to be controlled not by sight or knowledge but by faith.

Since every star differeth from another star, no bubble on the ocean, or grain of sand on the sea shore, or leaf in the forest has its counterpart, since facility and capacity differ by circumstances, there can be no hope for impossible unity. In the congress of opinion, therefore, we must yield concessions to our fellow man. No man knows all things. It often requires more wisdom to say "I do not know," than to say "I am right." Our estimate of the right and wrong we see in others is made up from what we ourselves are. In all our decisions the felicitous words of the great law- giver apply, "Let him that is without sin, cast the first stone."

Masonry, under whose auspices we meet this morning, is but little understood. It has existed since the days of the dim past, its head is crowned with the glory of age and antiquity, but its tenets and principles are such that they will never grow old or become out of date. At times in the past it has suffered at the hands of its enemies, while at others it has been popular with the high born and rich. Today it stands forth like a mighty army of men who form an invincible foe of many of the evils incident to human life. It wars against vice in all its forms, and it is ever ready to uphold the right regardless of party, sect or earthly power. It recognizes the good in moral, intellectual and spiritual man. Such lessons do our fraternity teach, such principles does it uphold.

Turning now to our text, we first recognize in God, the source of Light.

There are some things we can live without. We might exist without darkness. We can readily see how life would be improved upon if all trouble and sorrow were forever banished from human contact. I freely confess that earth itself would be a paradise if only sin with all its attendant evils were obliterated from its boundaries. These are things we can well dispense with, but while we can do without these, light is one of the many things we must have. Like the air we breathe it is necessary to our very existence. It is God-given, and like all that comes from God, it is good. Our first intimation of spiritual light is through the word of God. It was this word of God that was made flesh and dwelt among us in the form of the son of God. He has revealed the light. Through this holy book we have revealed God's law, God's light and God's love. Without this book we are in very blackness of darkness. Without it we grope on in blindness and despair with never a hope that the future may give a happier lot. Without the light of the Bible we are lost in a maze of doubt and spend our lives wandering to and fro upon the earth in a labyrinth of mystery that will end in eternal sorrow and ruin. Our greatest difficulties, no doubt, arise from our desire to thoroughly know and comprehend God. Many, because they cannot attain to this full knowledge, leave God out of their calculations altogether. Such persons only reach the level of the beasts of the field. They know not neither do they seek anything beyond the present. Given the present gratifications of passion and appetite, they simply wait for the demand to arise that the same passions or appetites may be satisfied again. A whole life thus spent is a life thrown away never to be of service to anyone, but self. In self, man will never find anything beyond self. Man as man never will be greater than man. Ignorance will never become knowledge, Darkness will never be light. Ignorance may and often does give place to knowledge. Darkness can be displaced and driven out by light, so man can step out of self into a divinity of life and acts that are ennobling. For this God gave us the light of reason, and a knowledge of what is right and what is wrong. Morality, through the light of God applied to man's life, can be set aside and immortality will take its place. This wonderful and desirable change can not be brought about by human agency alone. It must come from God. Our beloved order recognizes this great principle, and to God it gives the honor of being the source of all light.

Light is the source of life. The question is often asked, do plants grow in darkness. While this is disputed we know they grow in the light. Commensurate, therefore, with this thought that light is life, comes the development and growth of all that which is true and good and beautiful in man only as he dwells in the light of God.

Looking out upon the world of philanthropy, we see schools, colleges and universities for learning. We meet eleemosynary institutions, orphan homes, homes for the friendless, places of refuge for the fallen and destitute, hospitals for the sick and afflicted, and thousands of other like charitable organizations. Masonry, while not claiming to be the parent of all these, presents a title clear to many of them. It is a significant fact that all of these institutions, from the beginning to the end of the list, owe their origin to the law of charity and sympathy as taught by the Almighty Father of the Universe when he said, "Let there be light." The light of God, therefore, meant three things, *knowledge, love,* which is charity, and *sympathy.*

When God said, "Light be," he called into existence what may be denominated as *co-operative light*. Himself the great source of light, He did not intend that this great light should be for himself alone. It was given for man. God had no need of more light. Man is the needy creature. He is the one in darkness. The light was given that man might reflect God. We cannot afford to lightly esteem the power of associated influence. The ocean might be filled by a single drop of water easier than we can set aside the influence we yield. From the smallest atom to the greatest mountain, from the unmeasured realm that lies between space and matter, the unexplored region between fact and fancy, between time and eternity, in all of these we can not find a single object not dependent upon some borrowed influence. The sun shines, but it borrows its heat from some other source not yet fixed or named by human science.

Water seeks its level, but its very motive power is borrowed from the slope over which it passes, and the low elevation of the ocean into which it flows.

The cars rush through our streets, but only as they are compelled by the electric current that forces them onward. This current is dependent upon the motor which borrows its power from the heat generated by the coal. The coal in turn borrows its existence from the vegetation, the vegetation borrows from the earth, which in turn borrows from rain and heat and light, and which at first comes from God.

The necessity of knowledge in man makes him dependent upon the wisdom of others. "No man liveth unto himself." Man needs *friendship, advice, assistance,* and, need I add, *sympathy*. Did you ever stop to analyze this word sympathy? "Sighing with," not much in a sigh you say. Ah, yes, if it is a sigh from pure sympathy. A sigh for others' woe is worth more than 10,000 sighs for self. I believe in helping as we go along. We can do so much. A celebrated actor who had befriended a poor girl was laughed at, because she slipped upon the stage and handed him a flower. Rising in his manhood, he said, with startling effect, "You laughed at me because this girl handed me this flower. Back of all this is a sad story. I found her on the cold, snowy pavement, a little shivering piece of humanity. She told her story of a sick father. I went to his bedside because he was human—he was my brother. I nursed him back to life, and this child has only spoken her gratitude to me by this flower. I know you would pile flowers on my grave if I were dead, but I had rather have this simple token of love, this one flower, than wagon-loads of flowers piled on my grave when I cannot know or appreciate them."

God intended by this light of reason that we should love one another, and by our everyday acts throw flowers along the pathway of our fellow man.

Man's mission on earth is to reflect God in all he does. When God made man He made him in his own image. Is the image broken and destroyed? A small piece of broken mirror glass will reflect the whole of the sun. Only one condition is necessary. Turn its face to the sun.

The reason why so many lives are a failure is not because they are sinful, and broken like glass, but because their face is never turned towards God. "Men love darkness rather than light, because their deeds are evil."

Too many of us are moral cowards. We are actually afraid to meet the foe and fight the battle of life. We let the temptation of today overcome us, promising ourselves that we will be stronger on the morrow and that we will win the fight. Few men give up entirely to sin. There is always a misgiving. Conscience seldom sleeps long at a time. Our sin is ever before us. We cannot set aside the forebodings and fears as to the consequences of our wicked deeds. Oh, the folly of going to school and never learning—of always going hungry when the feast is spread for us— of remaining in nature's darkness when the light of God ever shines for us.

Let us determine, then, by the voice of God, that our life shall shine with a pure and holy luster. God has smiled upon us, and the sanctuaries in which we worship are often architecturally complete and beautiful, so let our lives adorn the doctrines of God in all things. To this end we must dedicate and devote ourselves to God. It is a question of personal resolution and effort. The light is here, but not for us except as we appropriate it and make it our own. As every individual determines the character of the mass, all depends upon what we are as individuals.

Remember that opportunity knocks at man's door but once. If not admitted then, it passes forever. This is a most serious thought. How many of us can look back and see drops of golden opportunities which we have allowed to slip from our fingers. Each day has its work. If you neglect a duty today, you cannot perform it tomorrow without taking time which belongs to something else. Be on the alert, for life is short, and time is fleeting. What is done must be done quickly, for ere you are aware of it your locks will be tipped with silver and you will be called to take your narrow chamber in the silent halls of death. Fight a manly fight and do your duty nobly, so that when the web of life is woven and the bolt of your earthly deeds is folded for shipment across the dark, mysterious waters to the shore of another life, you may feel the comforting assurance that when the roll is open to the light of eternity, it will bear inspection, and not bring us to shame. As members of this great fraternity, we are expected to do much. If our God would have us, we will one day open our eyes on a scene of glory— refreshment and our glorified Grand Master ruling among all mysteries.

NOTE

In the following sermons by Bascom B. Clarke, the writer employs a writing tactic, in which his sermons are all written in the form of a discussion or a lesson, to a fictional student of his, named Ezra. So, when you see that name come up, you may mentally replace it with your own name, or any other name you choose, if you like.

A Sermon About the Perception of Truth

Freemasonry, Ezra, consists of more than signs and passwords and mystery. The man who is no better off after he has seen the hidden mysteries of this grand old order that has lived through centuries, way back before the days of Saint John the Evangelist and Saint John the Divine, ain't got much material in him for constructing a mansion in "the house not made with hands."

Freemasonry doesn't advertise its business on bulletin boards along the railway tracks and in elevated stations excepting as the acts of its votaries tell of its helpfulness to man. Freemasonry doesn't maintain any lobbies in Congress, looking towards its own aggrandizement and how it may fasten its hold upon legislation, but by its good deeds, its upright acts toward all, Masonry grows in the hearts of mankind as it has ever grown since Solomon first wielded the gavel on Mount Moriah in the long ago.

Taking the obligations of Freemasonry, which teaches us to be good men and true, does not make us perfect Masons. You can't go through the forest without noticing many crooked trees, No matter how fine the meshes, you can't keep a "bullhead" from getting in your seine once in a while. It's not taking the obligations so much as it's living up to them that counts.

When I was a little boy I paid three dollars and a half, that I earned chopping cord-wood at six bits a cord, for book which the agent claimed would tell all about the "dark and shady deeds of Freemasonry." The man who sold me the book owned the wood-pile, Ezra, and not until I grew up did I fully understand his great interest in my welfare, but when I figured out that book-agents got forty per cent of the gross receipts, I could see how cheap I had chopped cord-wood.

Somewhere around the honey-bag in the bee's belly you'll find the sting. Whenever anyone tries to make you believe he's just honing to do you a good favor, you include hem and selvage in the shrinkage.

I didn't know a thing about Freemasonry back there, most fifty years ago, Ezra, and I wasn't in such great danger of becoming inoculated with it that I should pay three dollars and a half for being vaccinated against it. Well, I didn't read all the book, for it was tedious and sounded fishy in some ways but I got just interested enough to want to find out who lied about it, when I reached my majority. Here was this fellow going up and down the land peddling anti-Masonic tracts, and carrying a prospectus for getting subscriptions at three and a half bucks each for this "Exposition of Freemasonry." Here was his brother-in-law, with whom I had also lived, a superintendent of a shouting Methodist Sunday School. Well, the Sunday School didn't shout so much excepting in singing praise to God, but the congregation whooped her up, Lizer Jane, when the fires of religion got fanned a little. This brother in-law of the book peddler was a Mason. I showed him my purchase.

After looking it over he looked at me and said, "She may be good readin', son, but that little Bible you won in Sunday School that I presented to you last summer contains lots more truth." Then he looked at me, sorter pitying like and says, "You look over this list of our lodge members and tell me if you think they'd belong to an order that would do all the things that this book has laid up against us." That set me thinking, Ezra, and I said to myself that when I was twenty-one I'd try it and if I got by I'd know who lied. That's nearly fifty years ago this month since I walked over a little bare floor in a scantily furnished lodge room and learned my first lesson. Somehow, when they asked me the first question, "In whom do you put your trust," it was natural for me to tell them "In grandmother's God," and grandmother was a Methodist, not a shouting Methodist, but one of them still alarms that Masonry teaches about in every lesson. And instead of being invited to join a "gang of horse thieves," as they had been called to me, I found good old gray-haired Christian men reaching out their hands in welcome and calling me "brother." I was a little rat them days, Ezra, and two of the best old Methodist members black-balled me on my looks, not on my acts. One of them told this good friend who had taken my petition, "That boy ain't sixteen years old." I had to send way down home in Arkansas for the proofs and when they reached the lodge those two dear old friends, who had guarded the outer door, came and congratulated me and helped show me "the light."

Years afterwards when one of those old soldiers of the cross was on his death-bed I sat beside him many nights and helped care for him and received his blessing for it. He's in

Heaven now, and when I cross the "Great Divide" I'm going to ask him to introduce me to both the Saints John and other members of the craft.

I had to laugh a while ago, Ezra, when I was doing, a morsel of missionary work in getting some of the brethren's autographs on the dotted lines for the Consistory. It was for the Big Jubilee class, and I was making trips in the country in an auto, for some of the brethren lived far out from the city. One of these asked me how much I got of the initiation fee for my trouble. I told him "all of it and more too," for I was paying the interest on a debt that I had owed the order for many years. I was making up for what I'd lost on that three dollar and a half book that had caused me to seek the hidden mysteries I was seventeen years old when I bought that book. I've passed the three-score mark now and I'm proud of the fact that I'm a member of an order that helps good men become better men.

Just because the ignorant and intolerant say nasty things about Freemasonry, Ezra, doesn't make it true. There is no order nor church nor creed in all the world that is bigger or broader minded or more liberal. It needs no defense of mine.

A Sermon on Humility

It's mighty nice to wear Masonic jewels, Ezra. I used to think when I first inherited the right to wear the Square and Compass with that significant letter "G" in the center, that I was fortified to rub elbows with the biggest and the best of them. I wouldn't have traded my first Masonic badge, with what it meant to me, for anything short of a quarter section in glory. But badges only represent what is represented in the man who wears them!

If the brother who has been "raised" from the dead level to the living perpendicular listened well, he must have heard the beautiful lessons of the "square" and the "compasses" duly explained and every one of the twenty-four inches of the gauge representing the twenty-four hours of the day. If he heard these lessons only in routine and they made no impression on his soul, you couldn't exalt him very much by hanging as many badges and jewels on him as adorn the foreign diplomat, who comes over to this country to swap soft talk with our own crowd of statesmen, who shoot, "hit if a deer, and miss if a calf" in handing questions of state.

There's another thing, Ezra, that too many of us, who have received Masonic light entirely forget, and that's the significance of the letter "G." No Mason should ever forget the time when the Master called up the lodge and when all reverently bowed. Folks forget too soon, Ezra. The Mason who profanes God's holy name commits sin against his Lord and

Master, and a sin against his order, by aiding the profane in believing that Masonry tolerates profanity. Sorter think this over and try to skip the hard words hereafter.

In the old days, when I first saw the light, we were a tolerable poor crowd, Ezra, and had to do lots of scratching to get a little picking. Somehow, some folks sorter felt that being a Mason carried with it some supernatural power of "feeding the hungry and clothing the naked." There was a dear old brother in the little lodge back there who was always in church on Sunday and did most of the praying, but he was like some folks chopping wood, he couldn't get the "slight of using the ax" as we used to say in the timber. Try as he would, it kept him guessing what the family would have for Sunday dinner. One day he took ill and died, leaving a widow, who felt that Masonic jurisprudence included bacon and cabbage, wheat bread and potatoes, coffee and sugar, and plenty of it. One day we received a little note, including a bill of fare that was no slouch, Ezra. Most of us had been hittin' on three cylinders ourselves, part of the time, and to be invited to "sit in" and decorate the mahogany according to the widow's code was asking a whole lot. The worst of it was that this supplication came in the form of an ultimatum. She wanted bacon and cabbage and she wanted it in time for dinner that day. Ezra, were you ever so poor that a twenty-five pound sack of flour looked like the whole wheat crop of the United States, ground and bolted? Well, that was my idea of the situation when the widow wanted a fifty-pound sack. Fifty pounds of flour, Ezra, seemed like reckless extravagance, and me eating corn bread twice a day under protest! Why, the only reason I didn't pray the Lord to help me get a fifty-pound sack of flour — and me willin' to pay for it — was because I thought it was asking for too big a shake-down.

Anyhow, we held a council of war among the ten or a dozen members, and all of us together couldn't have created any flurry in Wall Street either, and we decided that having the name of being able to do the Multum in Parvo act, that it would be a shame not to maintain our reputation, so we levied an individual tax of four bits each on every able-bodied member of the lodge, and with this fund we sent a committee with the bill of fare to the last item on the list. We did more, Ezra. Realizing that if we received like demands every week or so, that the circulating medium which accelerates equine motion around the home base wouldn't stand the tension, when the widow in due course of time had put aside her mourning, and we found one of the brethren who seemed to have a corresponding disposition and who had been without a mate just long enough to have his wing down, we fulfilled our Masonic obligation of caring for the widows by boosting for the good brother in knightly style, until the twain became one flesh.

The gospel of Freemasonry, Ezra, consists in being ready and willing to strain a point, if necessary, to help those in distress. It beats all how much you can do after you think you've done all you can do. Just enter into your closet before going to bed, or if you are too tired to pray in a musty closet, why just lie down in bed — it doesn't make much difference to the Grand Architect whether you pray like a Presbyterian, standing up, or shouting like a Methodist like you thought the Lord was deaf, or whether you pray like the Arab, lying on your belly, just so you pray and mean it, old chap, — and before you begin to saw gourds for the night, sorter make a digest of the day's work and ask God to forgive you for the crooked paths and to help you plow straighter furrows next day. Pray, meaning it, and you'll sleep sounder, and feel better, and the help will come wherewith you may help others. But, Ezra, don't do like the fellow did who thought he was too busy to pray, and had the Lord's prayer printed and hung over the head of his bead, and at night, waving his hand toward the prayer said, "Lord, them's my sentiments!" Do a little stunt of originality now and then. It will help lots.

A Sermon on Obligations

Take your Bible and turn to the "Sermon on the Mount," as recorded in the seventh chapter of Saint Matthew, and you'll find these words, Ezra: "Not everyone that sayeth unto me, Lord, Lord, shall enter into the kingdom of heaven, but he that doeth the will of my Father which is in heaven."

I've attended lots of big meetings, Ezra, where they whooped 'em up until I have sometimes thought they'd split the shingles with supplications of prayer, and when the time came to seine the pond they'd get about all the fish excepting the minnows, but do you know they wouldn't all keep? Fish are queer creatures, Ezra. They are born into this vale of tears, orphans, are raised by the "daddy fishes" — their mothers consider their duty done when the eggs are laid. Well, human beings are like fish, and lots of Masons take the same view of the matter that the mother fish takes after depositing her eggs in the bed made ready for her. This class of Masons seem to think that paying the initiation fees and taking the obligations that entitle them to wear big jewels constitutes, creates and dubs them the whole works. It doesn't do any such thing, Ezra.

The spirit of deviltry takes possession of most of us at times, and I'm no exception to the rule. I'm not going to start in telling you what a saint I've been, and how weak the other "sisters" are. We are all human, some of us lots more so than others. I'm one of this kind. I once helped conduct a candidate through the solemn rites of the Chapter. I knew this fellow hadn't been building meetin' houses all his life, and I wondered how he slipped through the cracks, but he did. So when I got an opportunity and the Captain of the Host wasn't looking, I loaded him with burdens and told him it was according to regulations and he staggered under the load, until the Captain of the Host got wise. Then I got a lecture that was not in the ritual, but it did me a world of good, Ezra.

No obligation should be assumed lightly, certainly no Masonic obligation. If, somewhere under your rhinoceros hide the beautiful lessons don't strike the right chord, you've spent your time and money in vain and caused your friends to go to lots of needless trouble for naught. I once remarked to a Mason whom I had helped knight a Templar Mason, and in whom it did not seem to soak in according to my notion of things sublime. that a man who could pass through these solemn ceremonies without shedding tears had a mighty strong mainspring in his waterworks, but he told me that he hadn't noticed anything to cry about. Can you beat it, Ezra?

But I'm wandering away from the text. The Lord knew all about human nature and made allowances for the shouters and for the still alarms. He predicted that lots of men who had set up altars of Baal would try to get in the big show by creeping under the tent on that pica, but that it wouldn't work. There are lots of Masons who don't wear much jewelry and make but little fuss about their professions, but who go about doing the will of God and who follow the teachings of Masonry in their acts toward all mankind three hundred and sixty-five days a year. These may be scantily clad with jewels and emblems, Ezra, but they'll all have drinking cups when they come to the River of Life. It doesn't matter much where you start in the race, just so you press on, ever remembering that merit will sooner or later find its reward. Our Solomon was King of Israel, also the first Grand Master, and from the records handed down through the generations he was always ready to mingle with those who bore the burdens in building the Temple. Entered Apprentices always got as square a deal as either Hiram, King of Tyre, or Hiram the Builder, when it came to a "shake down."

I once sat at a Masonic banquet where men waited on the table. One of these waiters wore a Masonic jewel on his watch charm as big as the jewel of a high priest. It was adorned with a diamond most as big as a pigeon egg, and still he couldn't pass muster. It ain't the size of your jewel that counts, it's how sparkling a jewel you can become in the diadem of Masonic fame by your own good works which glorify your Father which is in heaven.

I'm afraid there'll be lots of disappointments about meeting friends up yonder. We'll have friends in both climates, but the question that concerns us most is which climate we're booked for, Ezra.

A Sermon on Building Character

Masonry teaches us to not only love the good among our brethren, but also the evil among them. Masonry was founded on common sense Ezra, and long before then I had become atoms in the world of thought or action, Masonry realized that most of us were human and some of us very human.

I've had considerable Masonic experience one way or another. It's not a bad place to pick up stones for the building of character, either, Ezra.

We think we keep the seine stretched well across the Masonic mill pond, with the meshes so fine that the dog-fish can't get by, but you've noticed that in the best screened sleepin' porches mosquitoers somehow do get through and nip you once in a while. It's so with men in every walk of life, and Masonry doesn't claim any supernatural powers or special charms that enable us to read human nature before its been tested in the crucible. We do our best, Ezra, and angels can't do more. You just turn back through the leaves of the New Testament, that Grand Old Book, that's mighty helpful to a man who is seeking the real old Simon Pure electric light of Masonic goodness, you just turn to any of the four gospels of Matthew, Mark, Luke or John, and you'll find out that even Jesus had a Judas in selecting the twelve. When you get to masticating these facts, don't feel especially called on to throw stones at those who may not have inherited your particular brand of hallelujah religion. For my part, Ezra, I'm strong on the Methodist way of praying. I have always felt somehow that the Lord couldn't help hearing a Methodist when he's hittin' on all six cylinders and using the right kind of gasoline. Still, just because I was raised on the "Upper C" kind of praying and preaching is no reason that a Quaker couldn't get a look-in because he uses the still alarm signals I once had a dear old Quaker friend who taught me my first lessons in selling machinery, and gave me the first real foothold in the business world. He visited me once, oh, he visited me several times for that matter, Ezra, but the first time I'll never forget how he acted when I nudged him to ask the blessing, 'way back there in that humble little cottage that I could justly call my own first home. I was taught to "read on my plate" or to have somebody intimate to the Lord that the menu was satisfactory and that our share was appreciated, ever since I can remember, and I'm glad of it.

I have a little grandson, Ezra, that folks say looks like me, and has leanin's my way. I taught him to thank God for every meal when his little lips could just lisp the words, and I'm strong on being thankful to God for his many blessings and mercies, and to all others to whom these presents come greeting small favors thankfully received and big ones in proportion. So when this good old Quaker at my table, I didn't just know how to go about mixing Methodism and Quakerism, but I knew that Quakers were generally very thankful for a good helpin' and this old boy was no exception. So I asked him to "open the religious jack-pot." He bowed his head and never said a word, but I kept my finger on the trigger until he raised his head, Ezra, and I knew he was through. I never felt that God had heard a blessing more plainly than he heard that which I did not hear, but which, like a drink of cool, refreshing lemonade on a sultry day, I felt clear down to my solar plexus.

As I said before, we think we keep the Masonic gearing well oiled, and the screens fairly tight, but once in a while we let a dog-fish in. Did you ever do much fishing Ezra? Well, there's something about it that appeals to me. The first dog-fish I ever catch bit little a yellow bass. He was a game old sport, to the manner born, and I enjoyed the tussle to the fullness, thinking that I had a great big yellow bass, but I was humiliated when I saw his nasty, slimy head as I reeled him in. To all intents and purposes he was a good candidate, and played his part well. He proved all that I could ask of a real game-fish, but he wasn't fit to cat. Do you follow me, Ezra?

Then, there's many a good Mason built out of what you might call ship-lap, in the lumber business. Why, I look back over all these years to when a good friend, "whom I afterwards found to be a brother," took my petition, and I have often wondered why. He's in Heaven now with that good old Quaker, and when I put out the fire and call the dog for the last time, Ezra, I'm going to visit them both and ask lots of questions. I thought it was because they needed the money. They had a square and compass cut out of sheet-iron, a borrowed Bible, that a dear old Methodist brother loaned them in the lodge, and the floor was as bare as a young bird's back in pokeberry time. But, Ezra, it was there that I learned lessons of friendship and the Fatherhood of God and the Brotherhood of Man that sank down deep into my soul, and which have helped me grow in Masonic grace, and in turn I have led others "by ways they knew not, and in paths that they had not known" and taught them the lessons at the "burning bush" where God told Moses to "Draw not nigh, hither, put off the shoes from off thy feet, for the place whereon thou standest is holy ground."

As I said before, I've had considerable Masonic experience in my day, and I'll tell you some of it now and then, maybe, if the hamstring of life doesn't break to soon I've heard the mystic words, Ezra, that cause men to fly over mountains and cross seas to render aid, and I've thanked God for this great privilege and for the associations with a craft that has shed the sweet fragrance of its helpfulness around the world, which has stood the sneers and falsehoods of the ignorant and of those before whom Masonry refuses to bend its knee or bow to their dominating will, and which has grown bigger and better all the way, despite these oppositions. I love this grand old fraternity that makes better men of those who were not so good when they crossed its portals, and which always makes better men out of good men. Selah!

A Sermon on Honor

Did you ever do any Masonic business on another man's credit, Ezra? It's not strictly accordin' to the code, but I once had the honor, if you could call it honor, of getting into a Masonic lodge on another man's credit. Well, it wasn't quite that bad, but the man who was with me was admitted on his brother's credit, and he could, of course, vouch for me, for I was Junior Warden when he heard the gavel fall the first time.

It was this way, Ezra. We were members in good standing of Plumb Lodge No. 472, Colfax, Indiana, and we visited Thomtown Lodge No. 113, located at Thomtown, Indiana. Now this brother who accompanied me was not only a brother, he was also a brother-in-law, and he resembled a brother of his so much that when we asked for a committee to investigate our Masonic standing and subject us to the "test," the chairman of the committee reached out his hand to my companion and said, "Why, you don't need to be examined, I can vouch for you." My friend quickly realized the mistake but concluded to have some fun, so he says, "Then I can vouch for Brother Sile," and here we went right into a lodge room packed with Masons, for there were three candidates to be "raised" that evening. We were invited to help confer one of the degrees, which we cheerfully consented to do. When we had finished eating fried chicken and other good things, my friend was called on to talk to the "boys." There's where the cat got out of the bag, Ezra. This "old boy" was no speaker in public, and his brother was, but I gave him the nudge to deal me a hand. After excusing himself and stammering around a while, he waved a hand my and told the Worshipful Master that I was some "taffyslinger," and, of course, they had to let me in on the deal. I had the cinch on 'em all right, and after criticizing them on their style of tiling, told them that two men whom none present had ever met in lodge before had passed the portals of the lodge without a test or a voucher, excepting by one not qualified to vouch for their worthiness. Well, they were no slouches at old Thorntown No 113, Ezra, and it required proofs to make the claim good. Then I told them the joke, and we all had a good laugh but no other fellow ever got by on his brother's credit in that lodge.

Then I had another rather strange experience years ago in Winnipeg. A dear friend and brother, whom I had helped conduct all the way from the Entered Apprentice degree to that of Sublime Prince of the Royal Secret, lived in Winnipeg when I visited him. Another good friend of mine from the States was taking his Red Cross degree the night I arrived in Canada, but this other friend could not attend the "Priory" that evening, so I strolled over alone, thinking that I might somehow convince them of my right to "sit in." I greeted the sentinel and told him who I was and where from. To my surprise, Ezra, the Eminent Commander greeted me most cordially and said, "You are just the man we need. We are short of workers. Could you act as Junior Warden for us this evening?" Could I, Ezra? and me Junior Warden of Old Robert McCoy that very year? I could. I told them so and in less time than I'm telling it, I was inside of a uniform and we did the work creditably. After the ball was over, Ezra, I asked them how I got in, and they answered by asking me the same question. There was no brother or brother-in-law that trip to help me out. But as I have said before and am about to say again, I've squeezed through some narrow places while pushing through this sheet-iron world, Ezra.

A Sermon on Acting Squarely

"Set a watch, Oh, Jehovah, before my mouth, and keep thou the door of my lips," from speaking aught against my brother, or against any man, even as far as it is possible to do. Think twice before speaking once, and if angry or provoked at another, think three times, and then say nothing for the time being.

There was once a man named Zerubbabel, who was chief of the tribe of the fathers in Israel. Masonic history informs us that when Jerusalem was made desolate by the Chaldcans, and Nebuzaradan, Captain of the host of Babylon, besieged the Holy City and wrought havoc with the Temple of Solomon and carried away the captives, Zerubbabel was among them. This grand old man must have had a worse time keeping the children of Israel in line during their captivity than Moses had with them in the wilderness during his forty years of wanderings.

Folks always find fault with their best friends, Ezra, when things go wrong at home and when trouble comes to overwhelm them. When you come to think about it, it's more of their way of entering a general complaint than of finding fault, but it's the time of bellyaches and no mistake. Here were the Jews, scourged and beaten, most of their men-folks killed off, the women outraged and their temple, the wonder of the world, that marvelous piece of architecture, laid in ruins; aye, more, the holy vessels of the Temple carried away and used by the profane on occasions of hilarity for feasting and debauchery.

Twas thus, when the yoke of tyranny had rested upon these forlorn people for "ten weeks of years." All this time Zerubbabel had been their staff and comfort. He was one of the faithful, one of the true blue, who flees not in the face of death, pestilence or disease, but who stands firm and by his example teaches others to do likewise. During his younger days, Zerubbabel was the friend and companion of Darius, the king's son, who made a vow that if he ever ascended the Persian throne he would set the captives free and restore all the holy vessels carried away to Babylon from the Temple in Jerusalem.

So it happened, Ezra, that when Darius had been proclaimed king, after their ten weeks of years of captivity, the children of the captivity prevailed upon Zerubbabel to undertake the hazardous journey of crossing the confines of the Persian Dominion and appear at the foot of the throne, in behalf of his people. This he did, having to fight his way part of the time and finally was captured and brought before the king in the garb of a slave, where, after some of the most trying tests ever given to man, he won by his strength of mind and unfaltering integrity the king's friendship and the freedom of his people, and by his brilliant address before the court of Darius he succeeded in placing woman above wine or kings and establishing the force of truth.

The point I want to make, Ezra, is that when we get in a hole, when trouble comes and overwhelms us, it pays always and forevermore to stand firmly and squarely by the truth. There are too many of us jumping cogs when the test comes. I've watched em with my own eyes, when the cider-press was squeezing the juice of truth out and leaving the pomace in the discard. I've watched 'em under the test and heard them hittin' on three, over facts that they knew as well as they knew their own names, and yet for fear of disgrace by telling the truth, they would take the other road, Ezra, and compound a felony by adding another to hide the real truth. The man entitled to wear Zerubbabel's signet, the signet of truth, should never lie but always tell the truth and shame the devil. You can squirm and dodge and beat around the bush, Ezra, and kid yourself that you've got through the bars, but that "All-seeing Eye" that looks down into the innermost researches of the soul, and which even the sun, moon and stars obey, knows when you are lying. And that isn't all. Around you are friends and neighbors who know your nature and your habits. Is it not better to have them say that you told the truth, even though it humiliated you to a certain extent, than to go away and say that you lied when the test of truth was applied? Sorter think these things over, Ezra.

I have always loved the example Zerubbabel set before the king when shown the treasures of the palace, the great bags of gold offered in exchange for honor, and finally the holy vessels of the Temple of Jehovah, carried away and profaned by wicked hands, even these treasures, including the Ark of the Covenant, how, when all these had been offered him in return for honor, he poured out his heart to God between the wings of the Cherubims for strength to withstand the great temptation and how God indeed sustained him. Suppose he had accepted the princely offers of the king and betrayed his people and his trust? He would have been scorned by the king and hated by his own, instead of returning to them honored above all others for his fidelity and made the king's cousin.

You know it pays to play the game square, Ezra. When you are invited to "sit in" and invest some of your substance in a few "seeds" that are hazarded in the draw, you always feel safer when you know that the little finger of the man who deals is invested with the signet of truth. Somehow, I'd rather lose my beans with a square man in an honest game than to pile 'em up at the expense of a gang of crooks. That may sound a little fishy. Perhaps it does to the man who "renigs" on a square question honestly stated by saying he can't remember, but it will go at par with all who play the game and pitch the ball squarely over the plate just as Zerubbabel did in the days of old.

A Sermon on Forgiveness

The spirit of Freemasonry emblazons the pathway of its votaries with kindness and wherever you find kindness and humility, where you'll find forgiveness stamped upon the brow of every true believer in the teachings of Freemasonry and in the practices of Christian virtues.

One of the first mottoes that Solomon dictated to his stenographer was "Mind your own business. Masonry has kept that motto stuck in its hat ever since, Ezra. Masonry plods along down the highway of life welcoming to its tents the Braham, the Jew, the Mohammedan, the Catholic, the Protestant and all the who are good men and true, to have and receive a part of its rights, lights and benefits, just so they are willing to be as broad-minded towards others as its teachings enjoin, whether they received their teachings from Confucius, Moses, Mohamet or the Founder of the Christian religion.

It's a mighty safe way of handling the human problem, Ezra. Why, if we were to publish every sign, grip and password, and tell everything that there is to be told about Masonry, the world wouldn't be any better off and Masonry would continue to be the power for good that it has ever been. Folks have pretended to tell its secrets, or pretended that others have told it all, but the God's truth about it is, that if every word was told few would believe it. Still, there are human beings who would give all they possess to just take their can-openers and pry the lid off and expose everything about Masonry, from its Bible to its billie-goat. I once knew one of this class, Ezra. You know that everything that has mystery about it is in some way by some folks connected with the supernatural. That's the case with Freemasonry.

There was a fellow living in the little village where I first saw Masonic light, who had what my good friend Mike Barry, of Phillips, once upon a time in the Kadosh, called a "yearning desire" for gathering in the secrets of the craft. The use of the lodge room was donated by a worthy brother, until such a time as the lodge could afford to pay rent, for we were working "U.D." and hittin' on three for lack of financial juice. In the ante-room was stored half a carload of hardware, pitchforks and shovels, long and short handled. The fellow with a bump of inquisitiveness as big as a goose egg confided to one of the craft, whom he did not know as a Mason, that he intended hiding in this pile of farm utensils and gain the secrets of the lodge. He further said that he knew they kept a goat, for he had heard it bleat, and he was going to watch the performance. Well, you know it doesn't pay to disappoint folks with a honing, Ezra, so when the word had been duly passed around among the faithful, we held what you might call a "clandestine meeting. By the aid and connivance of the brother who was hep to the game, we managed to get this "Cowan" properly hid in the "rubbish of the temple" at a meeting where no one in particular presided. We furthermore smuggled a bellicose and unruly goat into the lodge room beforehand and hid him in the other end of the hall. Now, this goat would as soon fight in a Masonic lodge as on the green sward, Ezra, as we had reasons to know. We pestered him until he was ready to take a header at whatever showed up. Then we called the meeting to order, but when we come to tile the lodge, the culprit was discovered as per arrangement. We held a mock trial, and concluded that he must suffer the penalty of the eavesdropper. Then things began to get serious, Ezra. The fellow began to realize that he was in a tight place. After much pleading and promising on his part, we blindfolded him to convey him from the lodge room without allowing him to detect our secrets. That's what we told him, but the facts were, Ezra, we wanted him to meet our goat. He did, he met him from behind, and if we had been using the finder and sighting for him, the goat couldn't have hit the bull's eye better. I've heard lots of cries for help in my day, Ezra. I've attended some mighty funny shows and helped exemplify some side degrees in the days of old, but I never laughed quite so loud or long as when that old goat hit Mr. Eavesdropper amidships. He plead for his life, which was finally granted on condition that he run for it, which he did. But our timer was still working, and he reached the door just as the goat did, and they both went down the stairs together in a catch-as-catch can mix-up, while all the crowd who had been armed with pitchforks and shovels hammered them together, creating pandamonium indeed. Talk about a circus in the Shrine, Ezra, we weren't shootin' at clay pigeons that time. Our inquisitive friend left town next day, for he said the Masons had him marked for death!

I suppose if we were to allow this kind of "carrying on" in a Masonic lodge today, we'd get churched for it, Ezra, but it was worth the risk, and not even the owner of the billie-goat knew that he had taken part in the initiation. When folks get overly anxious to pry into other peoples' affairs, and want to learn secrets in a clandestine manner, Ezra, it's a mighty good plan to accommodate them.

True Spirit of the Craft

And, whilst we are in this wise amending our past errors, and improving ourselves in holiness and godliness for the future, and thus walking in the Light, "as children of the Light;" let us not forget the Mason's Moral, to "go on unto perfection." O'er the tessellated pavement of this fleeting and checkered existence we are fast hastening to the common end of all men: and along the downward tract of Time we are descending, some more smoothly than others, but all with no less sure and quick transition. Let us not, therefore, be unmindful of the merciful ends of our Creation and Redemption, to "shine as the stars in the heavens," when raised in glorified bodies from the darkness of the tomb, we shall be presented by Our All-sufficient Conductor, before the Throne of the Almighty, and Ever-to-be-adored and worshipped Eternal Master of the Heavenly Lodge above! If, heretofore, irresolute and wavering, begin we, at once, to strive for the Mastery, that we may be perfect even as Our Lord was perfect; and in earnest to ascend the Ladder of Hope, by the regular and progressive steps of Faith, Love and Obedience. Our Christian, as our Masonic course, must be steady, gradual and measured, or our advancement in virtue and godliness will be irregular, uncertain and unsuccessful. This we have been already taught in the Creation of Light, and the perfecting of the visible works of God. And, even so is it in the Spiritual Creation of the soul anew. Our increase in Holiness, if we would come, in the unity of the Faith and of the "knowledge of the Son of God, unto a perfect man," unto the measure of the stature of the fulness of "Christ," is step by step, higher and higher, as we are enlightened, strengthened and improved, until the Door of the Grand Lodge of Everlasting Life open to receive us into the glorious abodes of Immortal Light. Oh, that we may, all of us, my Masonic Brethren, be the blessed partakers of that unspeakable and never-fading glory; and, to this end, may we remember, that we are not our own, but bought with a price; and, thus mindful, that our duty is to glorify God in our Bodies and our Spirits, which are His, let our Light so shine before men, that they may see our good works and glorify Our "Father, who is in Heaven."

A Sermon on Tolerance

By Bascom B. Clarke

I have learned the lesson of tolerance well in greeting Masons of many faiths because they were big enough and broad enough to exemplify the words of the text: Whoever shall do the will of God, the same is my brother and my sister and my mother.

The profane call us clannish, Ezra. Maybe we are, but somehow, in some way, I've always thought that Freemasonry was tolerably broad in its scope. You can always tell a man who has attended a big revival; he'll show it in his conversation and in his acts. If we could have a perpetual Masonic revival, lots of us would be saved. Those of us who have been dubbed and created as Sublime Princes of the Royal Secret, who have reached the summit of Mount Moriah, excepting the chosen few who are permitted to become Sovereign Grand Inspectors General of the Thirty-third and last degree, after the week of feasting upon the spiritual bread of life, after having been lifted higher and higher into the rose colored ether of the spirit world, when we have been permitted to hear the words of wisdom and of truth from the Great Sages and Holy Men of the past, from Confucius, Zoroaster, Moses, Mohamet and from the "Great Captain of Our Salvation," the "Prince of Peace," when we have had the beautiful lessons deeply indented upon the trestleboards of our hearts and witnessed those panoramas of pictures painted upon the canvas of our immortal souls, we come away filled with the "Gospel of Freemasonry, with hearts more tender towards the world and towards all mankind. But, somehow, it's human to allow the picture to fade, Ezra. I've sometimes wondered if it didn't pay to backslide, just to feel so gloriously good when we had renewed our covenants with God.

The Fatherhood of God and the Brotherhood of Man always sounds good to me, Ezra. If every man could fed when he took another man by the hand that he was a friend and brother, and if he could somehow make the other man feel the same way, we wouldn't have much use for jails and policemen, for standing armies and battle ships and cannon with which to kill and wound. We wouldn't have to take our boys from home and keep them on the Mexican border even for political purposes.

There are a lot of our boys down on the border now, some of whom are brethren of the craft. I had a letter from one of these, Brother and Sergeant Harry B. L. Gorman, of Company G. First Wisconsin Infantry. He's climbed the Masonic ladder all the way to the degree of Sublime Prince of the Royal Secret. He was on guard for Uncle Sam. During the meeting of the Consistory in San Antonio, Texas, wearing the uniform of his country, he sat with many other soldiers in the gallery on the opening day. Down on the rostrum, standing erect as a knight of old, was Judge William Seat Fly, 33d. Judge Fly, like your Uncle Silas's father and brother, fought on the wrong side in the war of Rebellion, Ezra, but he's one of the most loyal and devoted patriots living to-day, ready to fight for Old Glory if need be. With his hawk-like eye, Brother Fly swept the galleries of the Consistory, and seeing these brethren in uniform, he said, I want all you men in uniform to leave the gallery and come right down here and occupy these seats, referring to the seats reserved for the Patriarchs. You've got to give it to the Southerner, Ezra, that his hospitality is only exceeded by his willingness to fight for his country's flag anytime, anywhere. Maybe we are clannish, Ezra, but if it had been in any other place, and where it had been consistent with the order of things, that same proof of hospitality would have been accorded to every man wearing the uniform whether he was Jew or Gentile, Catholic or Protestant, because he was a soldier and an American. Thank God for that kind of clannishness, Ezra.

You show me a good Mason, one that has had it soaked in well, and who has the real old Simon-Pure spirit of Freemasonry in his soul, and I'll show you a man who measures up to the standard of manhood in every way. If there is trouble or danger or disease to face you'll find him right in the front ranks, whether that trouble or danger or disease threatens a Mason or any of the rest of mankind. Show me a cause that is just and I'll show you the men who will stand for it, whether those in danger are Masons, Odd Fellows, Knights of Pythias or Knights of Columbus, even though some of these faiths look upon us as "Spirits of Darkness." The true Mason is a true man, big brained, big hearted and always ready to lend a helping hand to uplift his fellow man.

Masonry carries on its good deeds in secret, because it believes in the still alarm. It used to be whenever there was a fire, the fire department began ringing bells and blowing whistles, and making more noise than a foot-ball game, but in these modern times the "still alarm" is substituted. Why wake up the whole city and get the people all worked up, just because somebody's oil stove has caught fire, when a silent alarm will bring out the squirt-gun quietly, orderly and do the work? Listen to this gospel, Ezra: "Therefore when thou doest thine alms, do not sound a trumpet before thee, as the hypocrites do in the synagogues and in the streets, that they may have glory of men. Verily I say unto you, they have their reward. But, when thou doest alms, let not they left hand know what thy right hand doeth, that thy alms may be in secrets and thy Father, which seeth in secret, Himself shall reward thee openly."

www.ingramcontent.com/pod-product-compliance
Lightning Source LLC
LaVergne TN
LVHW041500070426
835507LV00009B/718